An Important Person Has Died

Youth Workbook

A Grief Journal for Children and Teenagers Who Are Dealing With the Loss of a Loved One

Created by Dee Henderson

Copyright Notice

An Important Person Has Died...

This journal is written by:

It is about:

He/She was my:

He/She was born:

He/She died:

I was _____ years old when he/she died, and I am

_____ years old now, writing this journal is his/her

memory.

This journal is about my: (dad, mom, grandparent, brother, sister, etc.). Who were you? What did you like? What did you look like? What did you do? What do I know about you?

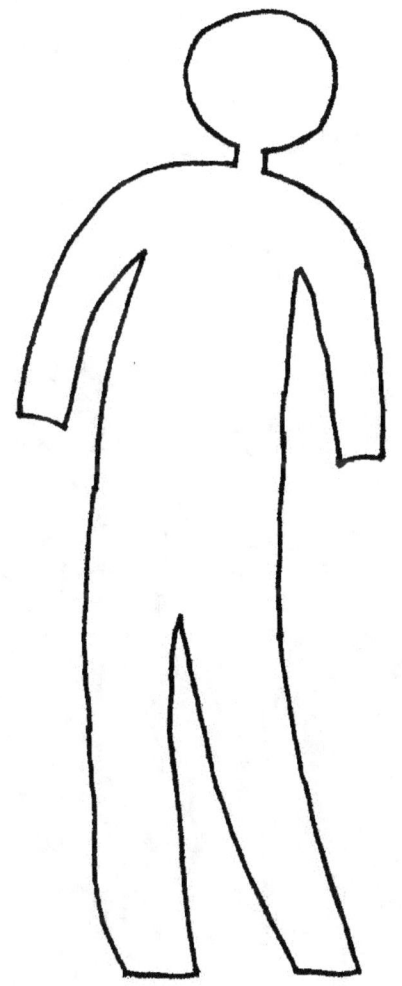

What did you mean to me before your death?

What do you mean to me now? How has your meaning to me changed?

What special things did we do together?

What were our favorite things to do?

The last time I saw you?

The last time I talked to you?

Some things about you that I want to remember always:

Things you said that I want to remember always:

The day you died, where was I? What was I doing? If I wasn't there, when and how did I find out?

My first thoughts and feelings when I heard that you had died:

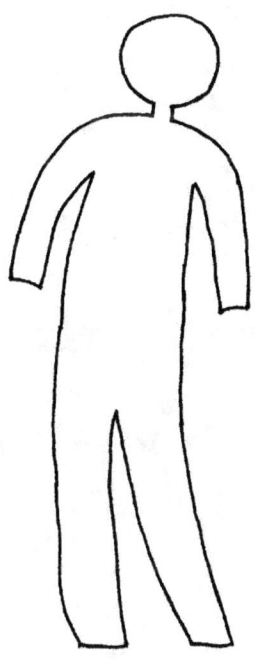

The details I know about your death: (time, place, how you died, who was with you, any other details)

Why I think you died:

What I would change, if I could, so that you would not have died:

Sometimes I imagine that I can feel what you felt when you died. What I feel:

If I could draw my pain, it would look like this:

What I have dreamed about your death:

Where and how I think you are now that you have died:

Your funeral or memorial service made me feel:

Seeing your body, closed casket, or cremains made me feel: (If I wasn't there, why not, and how I felt about that...)

If I could write on your headstone or urn, this is what I would write: (draw the headstone or urn, if you'd like)

My drawing or description of your funeral or memorial service: (If you weren't there, what do you think happened?)

I'm sad, angry, empty, and lonely for you... Other things I feel:

What I think other people are thinking about me:

A drawing of how I see myself:

What I hide behind my smile, good behavior, or even my less-than-good behavior:

Sometimes, when the rest of my world is sleeping, I lay alone and awake, thinking:

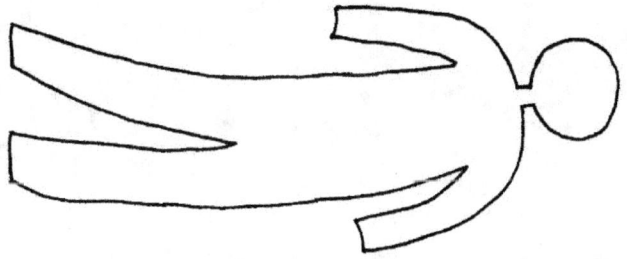

Things that bring me pleasure or happiness now, even though you are not here to share them with me:

People who help me to feel better, and how they do it:

People who don't help me to feel better, and why I feel this way:

Even though it wasn't my fault, I feel that I could have stopped your death by:

How my life is different without you:

Sometimes I think I can feel you near me. These things help me to feel that way, or remind me of you:

Something I have done, or will do, to honor your memory:

Drawings or descriptions of things I have that used to belong to you. This is how I feel about them, and how they continue to remind me of you:

Some things I wish we had been able to talk about or do before you died:

Things I want to tell you about now, even though you have already died:

Things that will happen in my life without you, and how I know that it will all be ok:

What I will tell other important people in my life about you:

What your death has taught me about myself:

You will always be special and important to me, so I want to write this goodbye letter to you:

Page Where You Can Attach Photos, Newspaper Clippings, and Any Other Things You Want to Keep

Page Where You Can Attach Photos, Newspaper Clippings, and Any Other Things You Want to Keep

Page Where You Can Attach Photos, Newspaper Clippings, and Any Other Things You Want to Keep

www.ingramcontent.com/pod-product-compliance
Lightning Source LLC
Chambersburg PA
CBHW071127280526
45787CB00003B/1194